AMAZING HOCKEY RECORDS

BY BRIAN HOWELL

Published by The Child's World®
1980 Lookout Drive • Mankato, MN 56003-1705
800-599-READ • www.childsworld.com

Acknowledgments
The Child's World®: Mary Berendes, Publishing Director
The Design Lab: Design
Amnet: Production
Red Line Editorial: Editorial direction

Design Elements: Shutterstock Images

Photographs ©: AP Images, cover, 7; H.J. Woodside/Library
and Archives Canada, 5; AP Images, 9; Jim Rogash/AP
Images, 11; Ray Stubblebine/AP Images, 13; Cal Sport
Media/AP Images, 15; Ryan Remiorz/AP Images, 17; AP
Images, 19; Gazette/Library and Archives Canada, 21;
Elise Amendola/Shutterstock Images, 23; AP Images, 25;
Ed Andrieski/AP Images, 27; AP Images, 29

ISBN 9781614734048
LCCN 2012946499

Printed in the United States of America
Mankato, MN
November, 2012
PA02146

Disclaimer: The information in this book is current
through the 2011-12 NHL season.

ABOUT THE AUTHOR

Brian Howell is a freelance writer
from Denver, Colorado. He has
been a sports journalist for nearly
20 years, writing about high
school, college, and professional
sports. He has also written books
about sports and history.

TABLE OF CONTENTS

THE GAME OF HOCKEY

Since the early 1900s, professional hockey has been played in North America and throughout the world. The National Hockey Association was formed in 1910. In 1917, the National Hockey League (NHL) was formed and took over.

Hockey has been a popular sport in Canada for decades. That was where the sport was invented. Many young boys and girls in Canada grow up wanting to be hockey stars.

From a young age, Wayne Gretzky was destined to be a hockey star. Throughout his childhood, Gretzky was a star in youth and junior hockey. At just 18 years old, he went pro. First he played for the Indianapolis Racers. Then he joined the Edmonton Oilers. That team joined the NHL the next season.

THE FIRST OFFICIAL GAME
On March 3, 1875, the first official ice hockey game was reported by the press. It took place on the Victoria Skating Rink in Montreal, Canada.

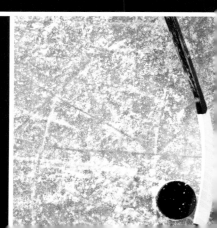

NATIONAL SPORT

Hockey is part of Canadian culture. There is a hockey rink in almost every town. They love the game so much, they declared it by law. In 1994, Canada made ice hockey the country's official winter sport.

Fans watch an ice hockey game in Canada in 1900.

For the next 20 years, Gretzky carved out a career that no player could match. He earned the nickname "The Great One." He proved why just about every time he skated on the ice.

As of 2012, Gretzky still held NHL records for career points (2,857), career goals (894), and career **assists** (1,963). Nobody was even close to him in any of his records. In fact, Gretzky's career assists total by itself would be enough to hold the career record for points.

Gretzky was an 18-time All-Star. He had his best season in 1981–82. That season, he scored 92 goals. He broke the old record of 76 set by Phil Esposito in 1970–71. Two years later, Gretzky scored 87 goals. This is still the second-most goals in any season. Through the 2012 season, it had been 19 years since anyone scored even 70 goals in a season.

During the 1981–82 season, Gretzky reached the 50-goal mark faster than anyone in history. He did it in just 39 games. Through 37 games, he had 41 goals. Then, he scored nine goals in the next two games combined.

Gretzky was truly a great player in hockey history. But many other players have managed amazing feats, too.

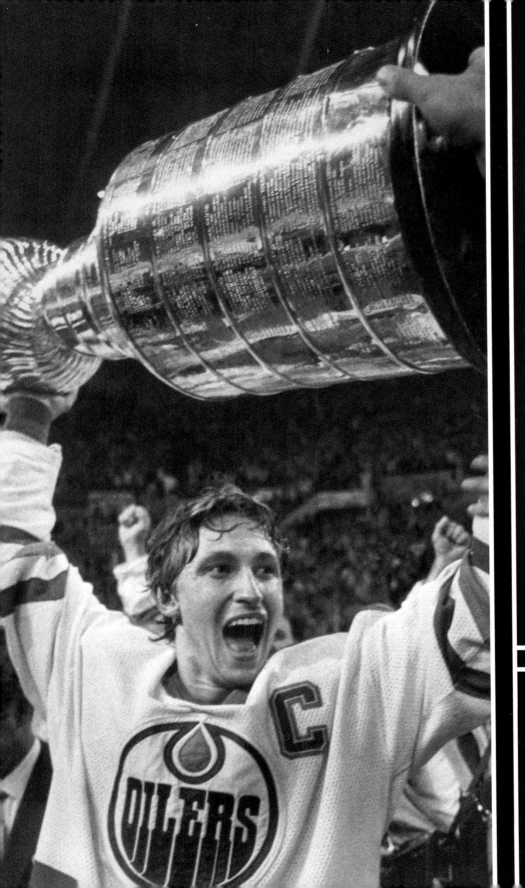

BACKYARD RINK

When Gretzky was six years old, his father built a skating rink in the family's yard in Brantford, Ontario. Gretzky skated on that rink as much as he could and polished his skills.

7

Wayne Gretzky lifts the Stanley Cup trophy after his Edmonton Oilers beat the New York Islanders in the 1984 Stanley Cup Finals.

AMAZING SKATER RECORDS

Gordie Howe was known as "Mr. Hockey," and it is easy to see why. Howe played in 32 professional seasons—26 in the NHL and six in the World Hockey Association (WHA). He is the only man to have played in five different decades: 1940s, 1950s, 1960s, 1970s, and 1980s.

From 1947 to 1971, he played 25 seasons with the Detroit Red Wings. In that time, he led the NHL in scoring six times, won the Hart Trophy six times, and helped the Red Wings win four Stanley Cup titles. The Hart Trophy is given to the most valuable player of the NHL's regular season.

PLAYERS TO WIN THE HART TROPHY AT LEAST THREE TIMES

PLAYER	HART TROPHIES WON
Wayne Gretzky	9
Gordie Howe	6
Eddie Shore	4
Bobby Clarke	3
Mario Lemieux	3
Howie Morenz	3
Bobby Orr	3

TALLYING 160
Only two players in NHL history have recorded at least 160 points in a season. Wayne Gretzky did it nine times, including a record 215 points in 1985–86. Mario Lemieux did it four times during his career with the Pittsburgh Penguins. Lemieux led the league in scoring six times. That included a career-high 199 points in 1988–89.

ALL-TIME NHL SCORING LEADERS (POINTS IN A CAREER)
1. Wayne Gretzky: 2,857
2. Mark Messier: 1,887
3. Gordie Howe: 1,850
4. Ron Francis: 1,798
5. Marcel Dionne: 1,771

Gordie Howe lifts his stick in the air after scoring the 545th goal of his NHL career in a game on November 10, 1963, to become the league's all-time leading goal scorer.

Howe retired after the 1971 season. In 1973, at the age of 45, he returned to pro hockey so he could play with his sons Mark and Marty. Gordie Howe played another seven seasons, winning two WHA titles.

In NHL history, Howe ranks first in games played (1,767), second in goals scored (801), eighth in assists (1,049), and third in total points (1,850). Including **playoffs** and his WHA totals, Howe scored 1,071 goals as a professional player.

BOURQUE WORKS BOTH ENDS OF THE ICE

The primary job of a defenseman is to stop the other team from scoring. Quite often, however, a defenseman has opportunities to score goals or assist on goals. Skilled in both areas, Ray Bourque won the James Norris Memorial Trophy five times in his career. Bourque was considered to be one of the best defenders ever. He leads all defensemen in career goals (410), assists (1,169), and points (1,579).

MOST 100-POINT SEASONS BY A DEFENSEMAN

DEFENSEMAN	100-POINT SEASONS
Bobby Orr	6
Paul Coffey	5
Al Macinnis	1
Brian Leetch	1
Denis Potvin	1

THE NORRIS TROPHY

Every year since 1954, the NHL has given the James Norris Memorial Trophy to the top defenseman in the league. Bobby Orr won the award more times than anyone else. He won eight times. Doug Harvey and Nicklas Lidstrom both won the award seven times. Ray Bourque is fourth on the list. He has five Norris Trophies to his credit.

Boston Bruins defenseman Ray Bourque (left) battles Dixon Ward of the Buffalo Sabres for control of the puck during a playoff game on May 9, 1999.

HOLT RACKS UP THE MINUTES

During his career, Randy Holt earned a **reputation** as a fighter. He spent almost as much time in the penalty box as he did on the ice. On March 11, 1979, Holt piled up more penalty minutes than anyone ever has in a single game. That night, Holt and his Los Angeles Kings teammates played a fight-filled contest with the Philadelphia Flyers. Holt received 67 minutes in penalties before being kicked out of the game.

During his ten-year career, Holt had 1,438 penalty minutes. While that is a lot, it's not even close to the all-time record. Nine different players finished their careers with at least 3,000 penalty minutes. Dave "Tiger" Williams holds the record with 3,966.

QUICK STRIKES

Sometimes in hockey it takes a while to score a goal. Sometimes it takes almost no time at all. On December 20, 1981, Doug Smail of the Winnipeg Jets scored just five seconds into the game against the St. Louis Blues. It is still the record for quickest goal from the start of game, although it has been matched twice since then. New York Islanders center Bryan Trottier and Alexander Mogilny of the Buffalo Sabres have also matched that.

SINGLE-GAME SCORING RECORDS

	NUMBER	PLAYER	TEAM	DATE
Goals	7	Joe Malone	Quebec Bulldogs	January 31, 1920
Assists	7	Billy Taylor	Detroit Red Wings	March 16, 1947
	7	Wayne Gretzky	Edmonton Oilers	December 11, 1985
	7	Wayne Gretzky	Edmonton Oilers	February 14, 1986
Points	10	Darryl Sittler	Toronto Maple Leafs	February 7, 1976

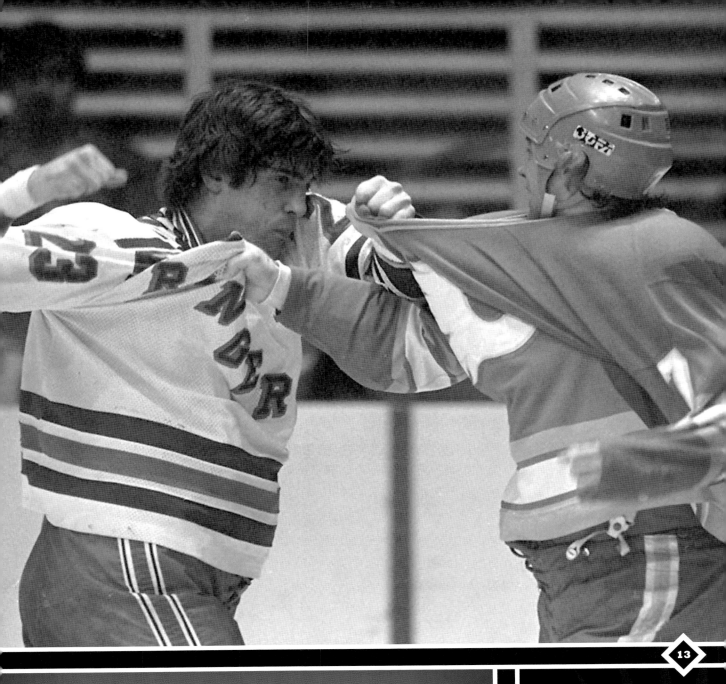

ALL-TIME PENALTY MINUTE LEADERS (CAREER)

1. Dave "Tiger" Williams: 3,966
2. Dale Hunter: 3,565
3. Tie Domi: 3,515
4. Marty McSorley: 3,381
5. Bob Probert: 3,300

Ed Hospodar (23) of the New York Rangers trades punches with Randy Holt of the Calgary Flames in a game on January 19, 1981.

AMAZING GOALIE RECORDS

There's no telling how many wins Martin Brodeur will have by the end of his career. By the end of the 2012 season, the long-time goalie of the New Jersey Devils had the all-time record for regular-season wins with 656.

Brodeur led the league in wins nine times. He is a four-time winner of the Vezina Trophy (given to the top goalie). He has helped the Devils win three Stanley Cup championships.

SINGLE-SEASON WINS LEADERS

PLAYER	TEAM	WINS	SEASON
Martin Brodeur	New Jersey Devils	48	2006–07
Bernie Parent	Philadelphia Flyers	47	1973–74
Roberto Luongo	Vancouver Canucks	47	2006–07
Evgeni Nabokov	San Jose Sharks	46	2007–08
Miikka Kiprusoff	Calgary Flames	45	2008–09
Martin Brodeur	New Jersey Devils	45	2009–10

CONNELL TOUGH TO BEAT

Alec Connell was an NHL star from 1924 to 1937. He played mostly for the Ottawa Senators. He holds two major records for NHL goalies. Connell's career goals-against average of 1.91 is the best in league history. He also has the longest shutout streak in league history, holding opponents scoreless for 461 minutes, 29 seconds. He recorded six straight shutouts during that streak.

New Jersey Devils goalie Martin Brodeur guards the goal during a game against the Washington Capitals on November 11, 2011.

ALL-TIME WINS LEADERS (CAREER)

1. Martin Brodeur*: 656
2. Patrick Roy: 551
3. Ed Belfour: 484
4. Curtis Joseph: 454
5. Terry Sawchuk: 447

*Active as of 2012

ROY DOMINATES IN PLAYOFFS

When he retired in 2003, Patrick Roy had won more regular-season games than any goalie in history. It was in the playoffs that he made his mark, though. Roy won 151 **postseason** games—by far the most in history. Martin Brodeur is second with 113. Roy went 151–94 in the playoffs. He had 40 overtime wins and 23 shutouts. He stopped 91.8 percent of the shots he faced in playoff action.

GOALIES TO RECORD 16 WINS IN A SINGLE POSTSEASON

PLAYER	TEAM	SEASON
Grant Fuhr	Edmonton Oilers	1987–88
Mike Vernon	Calgary Flames	1988–89
	Detroit Red Wings	1996–97
Bill Ranford	Edmonton Oilers	1989–90
Tom Barrasso	Pittsburgh Penguins	1991-92
Patrick Roy	Montreal Canadiens	1992–93
	Colorado Avalanche	1995–96
		2000–01
Mike Richter	New York Rangers	1993–94
Martin Brodeur	New Jersey Devils	1994–95
		1999–2000
		2002–03
Chris Osgood	Detroit Red Wings	1997–98
Ed Belfour	Dallas Stars	1998–99
Dominik Hasek	Detroit Red Wings	2001–02
Nikolai Khabibulin	Tampa Bay Lightning	2003–04
Marc-Andre Fleury	Pittsburgh Penguins	2008–09
Antii Niemi	Chicago Blackhawks	2009–10
Tim Thomas	Boston Bruins	2010–11
Jonathan Quick	Los Angeles Kings	2011–12

HAINSWORTH COVERS NET

George Hainsworth of the Montreal Canadiens was no stranger to shutouts. His 22 shutouts during the 1928–29 season is still an NHL record. His 94 career shutouts rank third all-time. Hainsworth set an amazing record during the 1930 playoffs. At one point, he played 270 minutes and 8 seconds without giving up a goal. That streak has never been topped in postseason play.

Goalie Patrick Roy celebrates on June 9, 1993 after the Montreal Canadiens beat the Los Angeles Kings to win the Stanley Cup.

ALL-TIME POSTSEASON WINS LEADERS (CAREER)

1. Patrick Roy: 151
2. Martin Brodeur*: 113
3. Grant Fuhr: 92
4. Billy Smith: 88
   Ed Belfour: 88

*Active as of 2012

Roy led the Montreal Canadiens to two Stanley Cup championships (1986 and 1993). He then led the Colorado Avalanche to two Stanley Cups (1996 and 2001). Through 2012, Roy was the only player in league history to win the Conn Smythe Trophy three times. The Conn Smythe trophy is given to the MVP of the Stanley Cup playoffs.

CLOSING THEM OUT

Goalies have played a major role in a lot of playoff games over the years. What Normie Smith did in 1936, however, was amazing. In Game 1 of the Stanley Cup semifinals, Smith and the Detroit Red Wings faced the Montreal Maroons. The game went into six overtime periods! There were 176 minutes of actual game time. That is just four minutes short of three full games. Smith did not allow a single goal. He stopped all 92 shots Montreal sent his way. No goalie has ever made more saves in a single game. The Red Wings scored the game-winning goal at 2:25 a.m.

FACE MASK HISTORY

Until November 1959, goalies only wore face masks during practice. But on the night of November 1, goalie Jacques Plante of the Montreal Canadiens changed that. During that game he was hit in the face by a puck. It opened a cut on his mouth that went all the way up to his nostril. After being sewn up by the doctor, Plante demanded that he wear his mask during the game. It was the first time a goalie wore a mask in an NHL game.

MOST SAVES IN A SINGLE SEASON
- **Robert Luongo:** 2,303 saves in 2003–04
- **Roberto Luongo:** 2,275 saves in 2005–06
- **Felix Potvin:** 2,214 saves in 1996–97
- **Cam Ward:** 2,191 saves in 2010–11
- **Marc Denis:** 2,172 saves in 2002–03

Normie Smith guards the goal.

AMAZING TEAM RECORDS

No team has experienced more success than the Montreal Canadiens. It is one of the NHL's original six teams. The Canadiens, nicknamed the "Habs," became a team in 1909. Throughout their history, the Canadiens have won the Stanley Cup 24 times. They won their first in 1916. From 1956 to 1960, they won five in a row. They nearly matched that in the 1970s, winning four in a row from 1976 to 1979. Their most recent Stanley Cup win was in 1993. That gave them 24 championships in 78 years. Through 2012, however, the Canadiens have gone 18 seasons without winning the Cup. It is the longest **drought** in team history.

LONGEST DROUGHTS
In 1994, the New York Rangers won the Stanley Cup for the first time in 54 years. That snapped the longest Stanley Cup drought in league history. In 2010, the Chicago Blackhawks ended the second-longest drought, at 49 years. In 2012, the 44-year-old Los Angeles Kings finally won their first Cup. Going into the 2012–13 season, the Toronto Maple Leafs had the longest active drought. The team had gone 45 years without a Cup win.

MOST STANLEY CUP CHAMPIONSHIPS

TEAM	STANLEY CUPS
Montreal Canadiens	24
Toronto Maple Leafs	13
Detroit Red Wings	11
Boston Bruins	6
Edmonton Oilers	5

The Montreal Canadiens play against the Detroit Red Wings in a 1959 game.

BRUINS IN POSTSEASON FOR 29 YEARS

The 1966–67 season was a bad one for the Boston Bruins. They went 17–43–10. The next year, they showed great improvement. They went 37–27–10 and reached the playoffs. That was Boston's first trip to the playoffs in nine years. It would be a long time before they would miss the postseason again. From 1968 to 1996, the Bruins reached the playoffs in a record 29 **consecutive** seasons. During that stretch, they won Stanley Cup titles in 1970 and 1972. The team lost in the finals five other times. The Chicago Blackhawks came close to Boston's record. They qualified for the playoffs 28 years in a row from 1970 to 1997.

MOST DIVISION CHAMPIONSHIPS

TEAM	DIVISION TITLES
Montreal Canadiens	34
Detroit Red Wings	29
Boston Bruins	27
Philadelphia Flyers	16
Chicago Blackhawks	15

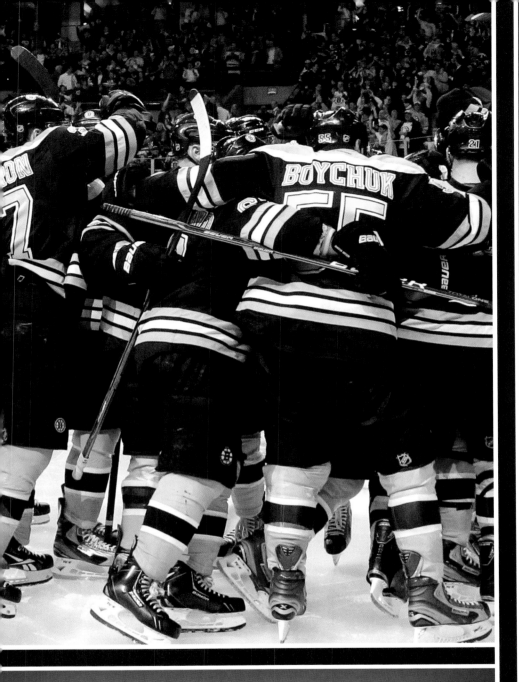

MOST TEAM STANDINGS POINTS IN A SINGLE SEASON

1. Montreal Canadiens: 132 points in 1976–77
2. Detroit Red Wings: 131 points in 1995–96
3. Montreal Canadiens: 129 points in 1977–78
4. Montreal Canadiens: 127 points in 1975–76
5. Detroit Red Wings: 124 points in 2005–06

Boston Bruins players celebrate their victory in overtime against the Washington Capitals in an NHL first-round playoff game on April 12, 2012.

FLYERS UNSTOPPABLE

During the 1979–80 season, the Philadelphia Flyers put together one of the most amazing streaks in sports history. The Flyers played 35 consecutive games without a loss. During that streak, the team won 25 games and tied ten games. That broke the previous NHL record of 28 consecutive games without a loss. The record also beat the longest winning streak in professional sports history. That streak was 33 games by the Los Angeles Lakers of the National Basketball Association. The Flyers ended the streak with a 7–1 loss to the Minnesota North Stars on January 7, 1980.

LONG STREAKS

- **Longest Winning Streak: Pittsburgh Penguins won 17 straight games in 1992–93**
- **Longest Home Winning Streak: Detroit Red Wings won 23 straight games in 2011–12**
- **Longest Road Winning Streak: Detroit Red Wings won 12 straight games in 2005–06**
- **Longest Losing Streak: Washington Capitals lost 17 straight games in 1974–75 and the San Jose Sharks lost 17 straight games in 1992–93**

JETS BREAK WINLESS STREAK

The Winnipeg Jets set a dubious record during the 1980–81 season. The Jets played 30 consecutive games without a win. That is the record winless streak in the major U.S. professional sports leagues. During the streak, the Jets lost 23 times and tied seven times. The Jets ended the streak on December 23, 1980.

Dan Labraaten of the Detroit Red Wings (in white) collides with Philadelphia Flyers goalie Phil Myre (31) and defenseman Mike Busniuk (21) during a 1979 game.

OTHER AMAZING HOCKEY RECORDS

The Colorado Avalanche had a unique season in 1996. The Avalanche was not a new team. They had played 16 seasons in Quebec, as the Nordiques. But prior to the 1995–96 season, the team moved to Denver, Colorado. It became known as the Avalanche.

Loaded with talent, the Avalanche won the Pacific Division in 1995–96. It ranked second in the league with 104 points. Then the team won its first Stanley Cup championship. It was also the first major sports championship win in Denver history.

Through 2012, the Avalanche was still one of only two teams in league history to win a Stanley Cup in

NEWEST TEAMS TO WIN THE STANLEY CUP

TEAM	YEAR	SEASON
Toronto Arenas (now Toronto Maple Leafs)	1918	1st
New York Rangers	1928	2nd
Boston Bruins	1929	5th
Edmonton Oilers	1984	5th
Philadelphia Flyers	1974	6th

Colorado Avalanche captain Joe Sakic (19) holds up the Clarence S. Campbell Bowl with his teammates after beating the Detroit Red Wings on May 29, 1996.

its first season in a new home. The only other was the 1918 Toronto Arenas. That team won the Stanley Cup in the league's first season.

MOSIENKO MAKES HISTORY

When a player scores three goals in a game, it's called a "hat trick." Scoring a hat trick is not easy, and it does not happen very often. On March 23, 1952, Bill Mosienko not only got a hat trick, he did it in record time. Playing for the Chicago Blackhawks, Mosienko scored three goals in a span of 21 seconds. It is still the fastest hat trick in NHL history. Mosienko scored 31 goals that season for the Blackhawks. In fact, during his Hall of Fame career, he had 258 goals and 282 assists.

HALL ESTABLISHES STREAK FOR GOALIES

Glenn Hall had a streak that may never be broken. In today's NHL, goalies rarely play every game in a season. Hall, however, played every game for nearly 8 years in a row. Beginning in 1955, Hall started 502 consecutive games in goal. It was a streak that covered all or part of eight seasons, two with Detroit and six with Chicago. Add minor league, All-Star, and playoff games, and Hall's streak was actually 881 straight games. Back problems took him out of play in 1962.

Chicago Black Hawks right winger Bill Mosienko holds up three pucks to symbolize his NHL record for the fastest three goals by a single player on March 23, 1952.

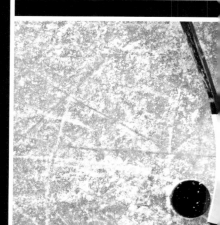

GOALIES WHO HAVE TAKEN A SHOT AND SCORED

GOALIE	TEAM	DATE
Ron Hextall	Philadelphia Flyers	December 8, 1987
		April 11, 1989
Chris Osgood	Detroit Red Wings	March 6, 1996
Martin Brodeur	New Jersey Devils	April 17, 1997
Jose Theodore	Montreal Canadiens	January 2, 2001
Evgeni Nabokov	San Jose Sharks	March 10, 2002

GLOSSARY

assists (uh-SISSTS): Assists are passes that set up goals. Wayne Gretzky holds a record for career assists.

consecutive (kuhn-SEK-yuh-tiv): Something that is consecutive happens one after the other. The Philadelphia Flyers played 35 consecutive games without a loss.

drought (DROUT): A drought is a long period without a win or success. The New York Rangers had the longest Stanley Cup drought in NHL history.

dubious (DOO-bee-uhss): A dubious thing is of bad quality. The Winnipeg Jets set a dubious record during the 1980–81 season.

playoffs (PLAY-offs): Playoffs are a series of games played to determine a championship winner. Patrick Roy went 151–94 in the playoffs.

postseason (pohst-SEE-zuhn): The postseason is the period of time after a regular season in sports. Patrick Roy won the most postseason games in NHL history.

reputation (rep-yuh-TAY-shuhn): A reputation is the way that a person or team is viewed by the others. In the NHL, Randy Holt earned a reputation as a fighter.

shutout (SHUHT-owt): A shutout is a game in which one team does not allow a goal. Alec Connell has the longest shutout streak in league history.

streak (STREEK): A streak is an unbroken series of events. During the Philadelphia Flyers' streak, the team won 25 games and tied ten games.

LEARN MORE

Books

Kirkpatrick, Rob. *Wayne Gretzky, Hockey All-star*. New York: PowerKids Press, 2001.

McFarlane, Brian. *Real Stories From the Rink*. Toronto: Tundra Books, 2002.

Wiseman, Blaine. *Hockey*. New York: AV2, 2011.

Web Sites

Visit our Web site for links about hockey records:
childsworld.com/links

Note to Parents, Teachers, and Librarians:
We routinely verify our Web links to make sure they are safe and active sites. So encourage your readers to check them out!

INDEX